JOHN JAMES
AUDUBON

· BIRDER'S JOURNAL ·

Pomegranate Communications, Inc.
19018 NE Portal Way, Portland OR 97230
800 227 1428 • www.pomegranate.com

Pomegranate Europe Ltd.
'number three', Siskin Drive
Middlemarch Business Park
Coventry CV3 4FJ, UK
+44 (0)24 7621 4461 • sales@pomegranate.com

Pomegranate's mission is to invigorate, illuminate, and inspire through art.

To learn about new releases and special offers from Pomegranate, please visit www.pomegranate.com and sign up for our e-mail newsletter. For all other queries, see "Contact Us" on our home page.

All works by John James Audubon (1785–1851)
Collection of the New-York Historical Society
Digital images by Oppenheimer Editions

Front cover: Western Tanager (*Piranga ludoviciana*) and Scarlet Tanager (*Piranga olivacea*)

Back cover: Black-throated Mango (*Anthracothorax nigricollis*)

Pomegranate Item No. AA309
Designed by Stephanie Odeh
Printed in China

26 25 24 23 22 21 20 19 18 17   10 9 8 7 6 5 4 3 2 1

CONTENTS

Introduction   4

Anatomy of a Bird   5

US State and Canadian Provincial
and Territorial Birds   6

How and What to Observe   8

Bird-Feeding Basics   10

Field Observations   14

Life List   115

American Birding Association
Code of Birding Ethics   142

WELCOME to the John James Audubon Birder's Journal! We hope that this journal will prove to be an invaluable tool for you to record your bird observations, whether you are a seasoned birder or a beginner.

John James Audubon (1785–1851) was an innovative artist and naturalist who documented American birds like never before. The dazzling watercolors interspersed throughout this journal were among the works included in his monumental work, *The Birds of America*.

How to use this journal:

Following the information at the beginning of the journal, you will find observation pages, which allow you to record all different aspects of your bird sightings, including when and where you see each bird and descriptions of the bird's appearance and behavior. There is also space for quick sketches.

Note that the journal pages are numbered. When you turn to the back of the book, you will find the Life List checklist of regularly occurring North American species. Next to each bird listed is a blank line where you can fill in the page number(s) of your notes for that particular bird. Then you can easily use the Life List to locate your own notes once your journal becomes more and more filled with your bird observations. (You can also simply check off birds on the Life List, whether or not you record any observations about them.)

Happy birding!

ANATOMY OF A BIRD

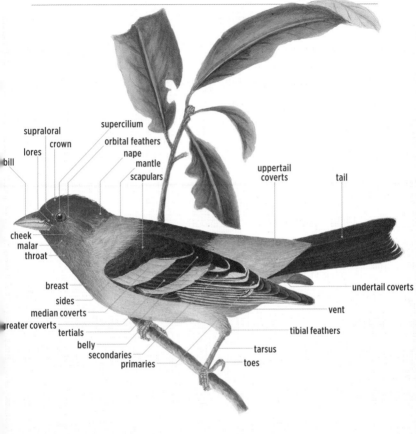

supraloral
lores
bill
supercilium
crown
orbital feathers
nape
mantle
scapulars
uppertail coverts
tail
cheek
malar
throat
breast
sides
median coverts
greater coverts
tertials
belly
secondaries
primaries
undertail coverts
vent
tibial feathers
tarsus
toes

IN SPRING the Barn Swallow is welcomed by all, for she seldom appears before the final melting of the snows and the commencement of mild weather, and is looked upon as the harbinger of summer. As she never commits depredations on anything that men consider as their own, everybody loves her.

—*John James Audubon*

Alabama	Northern Flicker
Alaska	Willow Ptarmigan
Arizona	Cactus Wren
Arkansas	Northern Mockingbird
California	California Quail
Colorado	Lark Bunting
Connecticut	American Robin
Delaware	Blue Hen Chicken
District of Columbia	Wood Thrush
Florida	Northern Mockingbird
Georgia	Brown Thrasher
Hawaii	Nene
Idaho	Mountain Bluebird
Illinois	Northern Cardinal
Indiana	Northern Cardinal
Iowa	American Goldfinch
Kansas	Western Meadowlark
Kentucky	Northern Cardinal
Louisiana	Brown Pelican
Maine	Black-capped Chickadee
Maryland	Baltimore Oriole
Massachusetts	Black-capped Chickadee
Michigan	American Robin
Minnesota	Common Loon
Mississippi	Northern Mockingbird
Missouri	Eastern Bluebird
Montana	Western Meadowlark
Nebraska	Western Meadowlark
Nevada	Mountain Bluebird
New Hampshire	Purple Finch
New Jersey	American Goldfinch
New Mexico	Greater Roadrunner
New York	Eastern Bluebird

North Carolina	Northern Cardinal
North Dakota	Western Meadowlark
Ohio	Northern Cardinal
Oklahoma	Scissor-tailed Flycatcher
Oregon	Western Meadowlark
Pennsylvania	Ruffed Grouse
Rhode Island	Rhode Island Red
South Carolina	Carolina Wren
South Dakota	Ring-necked Pheasant
Tennessee	Northern Mockingbird
Texas	Northern Mockingbird
Utah	California Gull
Vermont	Hermit Thrush
Virginia	Northern Cardinal
Washington	American Goldfinch
West Virginia	Northern Cardinal
Wisconsin	American Robin
Wyoming	Western Meadowlark

CANADIAN PROVINCIAL AND TERRITORIAL BIRDS

Alberta	Great Horned Owl
British Columbia	Steller's Jay
Manitoba	Great Gray Owl
New Brunswick	Black-capped Chickadee
Newfoundland and Labrador	Atlantic Puffin
Northwest Territories	Gyrfalcon
Nova Scotia	Osprey
Nunavut	Rock Ptarmigan
Ontario	Common Loon
Prince Edward Island	Blue Jay
Quebec	Snowy Owl
Saskatchewan	Sharp-tailed Grouse
Yukon	Common Raven

HOW AND WHAT TO OBSERVE

Using Binoculars

If you're not accustomed to using binoculars, practice with them by focusing on a stationary object. Look at the object—a distant tree, for example—with just your eyes first. Without looking away, bring the binoculars up to your eyes; find the tree in the lens, and focus. Once you've mastered still subjects, you're ready to move on to animals in motion. Using the practice method, focus on a dog, squirrel, or person, anticipating movement as the subject walks. Now try looking through binoculars at a bird. Predicting where the bird will fly can be difficult, but with practice you'll be visually tracking birds with confidence.

Using a Field Guide

One of the best tools for becoming familiar with the birds you encounter is by reading and repeatedly referring to a field guide. Photographs and detailed descriptions will be key in helping you first identify the birds you see, in your backyard and wherever you may go to watch birds.

Observations

When you see a bird, watch it. Refer to your field guide after studying the bird, as it may be gone quickly. Here's what to look for.

- Note the general impression of size, shape, and colors.

- Look at its head. Note markings, colors, and shape, and learn how to describe the bill shape. You can identify many birds by the head alone.

- Learn about the structure of the wing and note its colors and patterns when folded and when in flight; note patterns on the upper and lower sides.

- Note the shape and patterns of the tail, both folded and in flight. Look for differences between outer and inner tail feathers, and between base and tip of the tail, both above and below.

- Watch behavior. Where is it feeding (ground, tree trunk, branch, or leaf)? Describe how it moves: is it alone or with others of its kind?

The answers to these questions will help you figure out exactly what kind of bird you're looking at, even if the bird is very far away.

I CANDIDLY assure you that I have experienced a thousand times more pleasure while looking at the Purple Gallinule flirting its tail, while gaily moving over the broad leaves of the waterlily, than I have ever done while silently sitting in the corner of a crowded apartment, gazing on the flutterings of gaudy fans and the wavings of flowering plumes.

—*John James Audubon*

9

BIRD-FEEDING BASICS

More than one hundred North American bird species supplement their natural diets with birdseed, suet, fruit, and nectar obtained from feeders. Bird feeding can benefit birds and also provide great bird watching from your own backyard. The obvious time to feed birds is in winter, when natural food supplies are scarce; however, additional species visit feeders during the spring and fall migrations, and also during summer while nesting.

To keep birds coming back to your feeders in any season, provide them with the following three essential elements:

- Variety of quality seed.

- Freshwater for drinking and bathing.

- Ample cover, preferably provided by native plants. Native plants also provide potential nesting sites and a source of natural food.

Keep in mind that bird feeders also present potential risks, such as window collisions, predation, and exposure to disease. Following are some topics and tips for safely attracting and feeding birds.

Locate feeders at different levels ➥ Sparrows, juncos, and towhees usually feed on the ground, while finches and cardinals feed in shrubs, and chickadees, titmice, and woodpeckers feed in trees. To avoid crowding and to attract the greatest variety of species, provide table-like feeders for ground-feeding birds, hopper or tube feeders for shrub and treetop feeders, and suet feeders well off the ground for woodpeckers, nut-hatches, and chickadees.

Offer a variety of seeds in separate feeders ➥ A variety of seeds will attract the greatest variety of birds. To avoid waste, offer different seeds in different feeders, such as sunflower seeds, nyger (thistle) seeds, and peanuts. Black oil sunflower seed appeals to the greatest number of birds. When using blends, choose mixtures containing sunflower seeds, millet, and cracked corn—the three most popular types of birdseed. Birds that are sunflower specialists will readily eat the sunflower seed and toss the millet and corn to the ground, to be eaten by ground-feeding birds such as sparrows and juncos. Mixtures of peanuts, nuts, and dried fruit are attractive to woodpeckers, nuthatches, and titmice. Relatively few species prefer milo, wheat, and oats, which are featured in less expensive blends.

Provide suet during cool weather only ➥ Suet (beef fat) attracts insect-eating birds such as woodpeckers, wrens, chickadees, nuthatches, and titmice. Place the suet in special feeders or net onion bags at least five feet from the ground to keep it out of the reach of dogs. Do not put out suet during hot weather, as it can turn rancid; also, dripping fat can damage natural waterproofing on bird feathers.

Peanut butter pudding is a good substitute for suet in the summer ➥ Mix one part peanut butter with five parts cornmeal and stuff the mixture into holes drilled in a hanging log or into the crevices of a large pinecone. This all-season mixture attracts woodpeckers, chickadees, titmice, and, occasionally, warblers.

Fruit for berry-eating birds ➥ Fruit specialists such as robins, waxwings, bluebirds, and mockingbirds rarely eat birdseed. To attract these birds, soak raisins and currants in water overnight, then place them on a table feeder, or purchase blends with a dried fruit mixture. To attract orioles and tanagers, skewer halved oranges onto a spike near other feeders, or provide nectar feeders.

Nectar for hummingbirds ➥ Make a sugar solution of one part white sugar to four parts water. Boil briefly to sterilize and dissolve sugar crystals; no need to add red food coloring. Feeders must be washed every few days with very hot water and kept scrupulously clean to prevent the growth of mold.

Protect birds from window collisions ➥ In the United States, approximately 1 billion birds die from flying into windows each year. Protect birds from collisions by placing feeders within three feet of windows, if possible. Mobiles and opaque decorations hanging outside windows help to prevent bird strikes; or attach fruit tree netting outside windows to deflect birds from the glass.

Store seed in secure metal containers ➥ Containers such as metal garbage cans with secure lids protect seed from squirrels and mice. Keep the cans in a cool, dry location; avoid storing in the heat. Damp seeds may grow mold that can be fatal to birds. Overheating can destroy the nutrition and taste of sunflower seeds. For these reasons, it's best not to keep seed from one winter to the next.

Discourage squirrels from consuming feeder foods ➻ Squirrels are best excluded by placing feeders on a pole in an open area. Pole-mounted feeders should be about five feet off the ground and protected by a cone-shaped baffle (at least seventeen inches in diameter) or similar obstacle below the feeder. Locate pole-mounted feeders at least ten feet from the nearest shrub, tree, or other tall structure.

Keep cats indoors ➻ Cats kill hundreds of millions of birds annually in the United States, often pouncing on ground-feeding birds and those dazed by window collisions. Responsible and caring cat owners keep their cats indoors, where they are also safer from traffic, disease, and fights with other animals. Outdoor cats are especially dangerous to birds in the spring, when fledglings are on the ground. Bells on cat collars are usually ineffective for deterring predation.

Clean feeders and rake up spilled grain and hulls ➻ Uneaten seed can become soggy and grow deadly mold. Empty and clean feeders twice a year (spring and fall), more often if feeders are used during humid summers. Using a long-handled bottlebrush, scrub with dish detergent and rinse with a powerful hose; then soak in a bucket of 10 percent non-chlorine bleach solution, rinse well, and dry in the sun. In early spring, rake up spilled grain and sunflower hulls.

I THINK I can safely venture to say I have seen not fewer than ten thousand of these birds [Black Skimmers] in a single flock.

—*John James Audubon*

1 Anna's Hummingbird (*Calypte anna*)

3 Clark's Nutcracker (*Nucifraga columbiana*)

5 Western Tanager (*Piranga ludoviciana*)

6 Northern Parula (*Parula americana*)

9 Northern Cardinal (*Cardinalis cardinalis*)

12 Black-billed Magpie (*Pica pica*)

14 Merlin *(Falco columbarius)*

19 American Robin (*Turdus migratorius*)

22 Eastern Bluebird (*Sialia sialis*)

26 King Eider (*Somateria spectabilis*)

30 Wild Turkey (*Meleagris gallopavo*)

35 Bachman's Sparrow (*Aimophila aestivalis*)

38 White Ibis (*Eudocimus albus*)

43 Gray Kingbird (*Tyrannus dominicensis*)

46 Vesper Sparrow (*Pooecetes gramineus*)

51 Nashville Warbler (*Vermivora ruficapilla*)

54 Black-backed Woodpecker (*Picoides arcticus*)

58 American Robin (*Turdus migratorius*)

62 Black-billed Magpie (*Pica pica*)

67 Tufted Puffin (*Fratercula cirrhata*)

70 Red-bellied Woodpecker (*Melanerpes carolinus*), Northern Flicker (*Colaptes auratus*), Red-breasted Sapsucker (*Sphyrapicus ruber*), Lewis's Woodpecker (*Melanerpes lewis*), and Hairy Woodpecker (*Picoides villosus*)

74 Band-tailed Pigeon (*Columba fasciata*)

78 Blue-winged Teal (*Anas discors*)

83 Painted Bunting (*Passerina ciris*)

86 Great Horned Owl (*Bubo virginianus*)

90 Yellow-billed Magpie (*Pica nuttalli*), Steller's Jay (*Cyanocitta stelleri*), Western Scrub-Jay (*Aphelocoma californica*), Clark's Nutcracker (*Nucifraga columbiana*)

95 Great Crested Flycatcher (*Myiarchus crinitus*)

98 Purple Gallinule (*Porphyrula martinica*)

102 Bachman's Warbler *(Vermivora bachmanii)*

105 Acadian Flycatcher (*Empidonax virescens*)

114 Blue-winged Warbler (*Vermivora pinus*)

141 Blue-headed Quail-dove (*Starnoenas cyanocephala*)

144 Townsend's Warbler (*Dendroica townsendi*), Audubon's Warbler (*Dendroica coronata auduboni*), Mountain Bluebird (*Sialia currucoides*), Western Bluebird (*Sialia mexicana*), Black-throated Gray Warbler (*Dendroica nigrescens*), and Hermit Warbler (*Dendroica occidentalis*)

FIELD OBSERVATIONS

DATE/TIME OF DAY

LOCATION

WEATHER

SPECIES/DESCRIPTION

ACCOMPANIED BY

OBSERVATIONS

NOTES

SKETCHES

FIELD OBSERVATIONS

DATE/TIME OF DAY

LOCATION

WEATHER

SPECIES/DESCRIPTION

ACCOMPANIED BY

OBSERVATIONS

NOTES

SKETCHES

FIELD OBSERVATIONS

DATE/TIME OF DAY

LOCATION

WEATHER

SPECIES/DESCRIPTION

ACCOMPANIED BY

OBSERVATIONS

NOTES

SKETCHES

FIELD OBSERVATIONS

DATE/TIME OF DAY

LOCATION

WEATHER

SPECIES/DESCRIPTION

ACCOMPANIED BY

OBSERVATIONS

NOTES

SKETCHES

FIELD OBSERVATIONS

DATE/TIME OF DAY

LOCATION

WEATHER

SPECIES/DESCRIPTION

ACCOMPANIED BY

OBSERVATIONS

NOTES

SKETCHES

FIELD OBSERVATIONS

DATE/TIME OF DAY

LOCATION

WEATHER

SPECIES/DESCRIPTION

ACCOMPANIED BY

OBSERVATIONS

NOTES

SKETCHES

FIELD OBSERVATIONS

DATE/TIME OF DAY

LOCATION

WEATHER

SPECIES/DESCRIPTION

ACCOMPANIED BY

OBSERVATIONS

NOTES

SKETCHES

EXCEPTING OUR little partridge, I know of no small bird so swift of foot as the Virginia Rail. In fact, I doubt if it would be an easy matter for an active man to outstrip one of them on plain ground and to trust to one's speed for raising one among the thick herbage to which they usually resort.

—*John James Audubon*

FIELD OBSERVATIONS

DATE/TIME OF DAY

LOCATION

WEATHER

SPECIES/DESCRIPTION

ACCOMPANIED BY

OBSERVATIONS

NOTES

SKETCHES

FIELD OBSERVATIONS

DATE/TIME OF DAY

LOCATION

WEATHER

SPECIES/DESCRIPTION

ACCOMPANIED BY

OBSERVATIONS

NOTES

SKETCHES

FIELD OBSERVATIONS

DATE/TIME OF DAY

LOCATION

WEATHER

SPECIES/DESCRIPTION

ACCOMPANIED BY

OBSERVATIONS

NOTES

SKETCHES

FIELD OBSERVATIONS

DATE/TIME OF DAY

LOCATION

WEATHER

SPECIES/DESCRIPTION

ACCOMPANIED BY

OBSERVATIONS

NOTES

SKETCHES

IT [the Greater Yellowlegs (Tell-tale Godwit or Snipe)] is a cunning and watchful bird, ever willing to admonish you or me, or any other person whom it may observe advancing towards it with no good intent. . . . The Telltale merely intends by its cries to preserve itself, and not generously to warn others of their danger.

—John James Audubon

FIELD OBSERVATIONS

DATE/TIME OF DAY

LOCATION

WEATHER

SPECIES/DESCRIPTION

ACCOMPANIED BY

OBSERVATIONS

NOTES

SKETCHES

FIELD OBSERVATIONS

DATE/TIME OF DAY

LOCATION

WEATHER

SPECIES/DESCRIPTION

ACCOMPANIED BY

OBSERVATIONS

NOTES

SKETCHES

FIELD OBSERVATIONS

DATE/TIME OF DAY

LOCATION

WEATHER

SPECIES/DESCRIPTION

ACCOMPANIED BY

OBSERVATIONS

NOTES

SKETCHES

FIELD OBSERVATIONS

DATE/TIME OF DAY

LOCATION

WEATHER

SPECIES/DESCRIPTION

ACCOMPANIED BY

OBSERVATIONS

NOTES

SKETCHES

FIELD OBSERVATIONS

DATE/TIME OF DAY

LOCATION

WEATHER

SPECIES/DESCRIPTION

ACCOMPANIED BY

OBSERVATIONS

NOTES

SKETCHES

FIELD OBSERVATIONS

DATE/TIME OF DAY

LOCATION

WEATHER

SPECIES/DESCRIPTION

ACCOMPANIED BY

OBSERVATIONS

NOTES

SKETCHES

FIELD OBSERVATIONS

DATE/TIME OF DAY

LOCATION

WEATHER

SPECIES/DESCRIPTION

ACCOMPANIED BY

OBSERVATIONS

NOTES

SKETCHES

FIELD OBSERVATIONS

DATE/TIME OF DAY

LOCATION

WEATHER

SPECIES/DESCRIPTION

ACCOMPANIED BY

OBSERVATIONS

NOTES

SKETCHES

FIELD OBSERVATIONS

DATE/TIME OF DAY

LOCATION

WEATHER

SPECIES/DESCRIPTION

ACCOMPANIED BY

OBSERVATIONS

NOTES

SKETCHES

FIELD OBSERVATIONS

DATE/TIME OF DAY

LOCATION

WEATHER

SPECIES/DESCRIPTION

ACCOMPANIED BY

OBSERVATIONS

NOTES

SKETCHES

FIELD OBSERVATIONS

DATE/TIME OF DAY

LOCATION

WEATHER

SPECIES/DESCRIPTION

ACCOMPANIED BY

OBSERVATIONS

NOTES

SKETCHES

FIELD OBSERVATIONS

DATE/TIME OF DAY

LOCATION

WEATHER

SPECIES/DESCRIPTION

ACCOMPANIED BY

OBSERVATIONS

NOTES

SKETCHES

WITH AN easy and buoyant flight, the Tern [Common Tern (Great Tern)] visits the whole of our indented coast . . . amidst all the comforts and enjoyments which kind nature has provided for it. Full of agreeable sensations, the mated pair glide along side by side, as gaily as ever a bridegroom and bride. The air is warm, the sky of purest azure, and in every nook the glittering fry tempts to satiate their appetite.

—John James Audubon

FIELD OBSERVATIONS

DATE/TIME OF DAY

LOCATION

WEATHER

SPECIES/DESCRIPTION

ACCOMPANIED BY

OBSERVATIONS

NOTES

SKETCHES

FIELD OBSERVATIONS

DATE/TIME OF DAY

LOCATION

WEATHER

SPECIES/DESCRIPTION

ACCOMPANIED BY

OBSERVATIONS

NOTES

SKETCHES

FIELD OBSERVATIONS

DATE/TIME OF DAY

LOCATION

WEATHER

SPECIES/DESCRIPTION

ACCOMPANIED BY

OBSERVATIONS

NOTES

SKETCHES

FIELD OBSERVATIONS

DATE/TIME OF DAY

LOCATION

WEATHER

SPECIES/DESCRIPTION

ACCOMPANIED BY

OBSERVATIONS

NOTES

SKETCHES

FIELD OBSERVATIONS

DATE/TIME OF DAY

LOCATION

WEATHER

SPECIES/DESCRIPTION

ACCOMPANIED BY

OBSERVATIONS

NOTES

SKETCHES

FIELD OBSERVATIONS

DATE/TIME OF DAY

LOCATION

WEATHER

SPECIES/DESCRIPTION

ACCOMPANIED BY

OBSERVATIONS

NOTES

SKETCHES

FIELD OBSERVATIONS

DATE/TIME OF DAY

LOCATION

WEATHER

SPECIES/DESCRIPTION

ACCOMPANIED BY

OBSERVATIONS

NOTES

SKETCHES

FIELD OBSERVATIONS

DATE/TIME OF DAY

LOCATION

WEATHER

SPECIES/DESCRIPTION

ACCOMPANIED BY

OBSERVATIONS

NOTES

SKETCHES

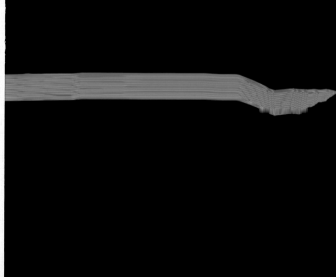

FIELD OBSERVATIONS

DATE/TIME OF DAY

LOCATION

WEATHER

SPECIES/DESCRIPTION

ACCOMPANIED BY

OBSERVATIONS

NOTES

SKETCHES

FIELD OBSERVATIONS

DATE/TIME OF DAY

LOCATION

WEATHER

SPECIES/DESCRIPTION

ACCOMPANIED BY

OBSERVATIONS

NOTES

SKETCHES

FIELD OBSERVATIONS

DATE/TIME OF DAY

LOCATION

WEATHER

SPECIES/DESCRIPTION

ACCOMPANIED BY

OBSERVATIONS

NOTES

SKETCHES

FIELD OBSERVATIONS

DATE/TIME OF DAY

LOCATION

WEATHER

SPECIES/DESCRIPTION

ACCOMPANIED BY

OBSERVATIONS

NOTES

SKETCHES

FIELD OBSERVATIONS

DATE/TIME OF DAY

LOCATION

WEATHER

SPECIES/DESCRIPTION

ACCOMPANIED BY

OBSERVATIONS

NOTES

SKETCHES

FIELD OBSERVATIONS

DATE/TIME OF DAY

LOCATION

WEATHER

SPECIES/DESCRIPTION

ACCOMPANIED BY

OBSERVATIONS

NOTES

SKETCHES

NOTHING CAN exceed the lightness of the flight of this bird [Little Tern (Lesser Tern)], which seems to me to be among water-fowls, the analogue of the Hummingbird. Hovering on rapidly beating wings it spots its tiny finny prey and dives upon it with the quickness of thought.

—John James Audubon

FIELD OBSERVATIONS

DATE/TIME OF DAY

LOCATION

WEATHER

SPECIES/DESCRIPTION

ACCOMPANIED BY

OBSERVATIONS

NOTES

SKETCHES

FIELD OBSERVATIONS

DATE/TIME OF DAY

LOCATION

WEATHER

SPECIES/DESCRIPTION

ACCOMPANIED BY

OBSERVATIONS

NOTES

SKETCHES

FIELD OBSERVATIONS

DATE/TIME OF DAY

LOCATION

WEATHER

SPECIES/DESCRIPTION

ACCOMPANIED BY

OBSERVATIONS

NOTES

SKETCHES

FIELD OBSERVATIONS

DATE/TIME OF DAY

LOCATION

WEATHER

SPECIES/DESCRIPTION

ACCOMPANIED BY

OBSERVATIONS

NOTES

SKETCHES

FIELD OBSERVATIONS

DATE/TIME OF DAY _____

LOCATION _____

WEATHER _____

SPECIES/DESCRIPTION _____

_____

ACCOMPANIED BY _____

OBSERVATIONS _____

_____

NOTES _____

_____

_____

SKETCHES

FIELD OBSERVATIONS

DATE/TIME OF DAY

LOCATION

WEATHER

SPECIES/DESCRIPTION

ACCOMPANIED BY

OBSERVATIONS

NOTES

SKETCHES

FIELD OBSERVATIONS

DATE/TIME OF DAY

LOCATION

WEATHER

SPECIES/DESCRIPTION

ACCOMPANIED BY

OBSERVATIONS

NOTES

SKETCHES

FIELD OBSERVATIONS

DATE/TIME OF DAY

LOCATION

WEATHER

SPECIES/DESCRIPTION

ACCOMPANIED BY

OBSERVATIONS

NOTES

SKETCHES

FIELD OBSERVATIONS

DATE/TIME OF DAY

LOCATION

WEATHER

SPECIES/DESCRIPTION

ACCOMPANIED BY

OBSERVATIONS

NOTES

SKETCHES

FIELD OBSERVATIONS

DATE/TIME OF DAY

LOCATION

WEATHER

SPECIES/DESCRIPTION

ACCOMPANIED BY

OBSERVATIONS

NOTES

SKETCHES

FIELD OBSERVATIONS

DATE/TIME OF DAY

LOCATION

WEATHER

SPECIES/DESCRIPTION

ACCOMPANIED BY

OBSERVATIONS

NOTES

SKETCHES

FIELD OBSERVATIONS

DATE/TIME OF DAY

LOCATION

WEATHER

SPECIES/DESCRIPTION

ACCOMPANIED BY

OBSERVATIONS

NOTES

SKETCHES

THE ZENAIDA Dove is a transient visitor of the Keys of East Florida. . . . Heard in the wildest solitudes [its] notes never fail to remind one that he is in the presence and under the protection of the Almighty Creator.

—*John James Audubon*

FIELD OBSERVATIONS

DATE/TIME OF DAY

LOCATION

WEATHER

SPECIES/DESCRIPTION

ACCOMPANIED BY

OBSERVATIONS

NOTES

SKETCHES

FIELD OBSERVATIONS

DATE/TIME OF DAY

LOCATION

WEATHER

SPECIES/DESCRIPTION

ACCOMPANIED BY

OBSERVATIONS

NOTES

SKETCHES

FIELD OBSERVATIONS

DATE/TIME OF DAY

LOCATION

WEATHER

SPECIES/DESCRIPTION

ACCOMPANIED BY

OBSERVATIONS

NOTES

SKETCHES

FIELD OBSERVATIONS

DATE/TIME OF DAY

LOCATION

WEATHER

SPECIES/DESCRIPTION

ACCOMPANIED BY

OBSERVATIONS

NOTES

SKETCHES

FIELD OBSERVATIONS

DATE/TIME OF DAY

LOCATION

WEATHER

SPECIES/DESCRIPTION

ACCOMPANIED BY

OBSERVATIONS

NOTES

SKETCHES

FIELD OBSERVATIONS

DATE/TIME OF DAY

LOCATION

WEATHER

SPECIES/DESCRIPTION

ACCOMPANIED BY

OBSERVATIONS

NOTES

SKETCHES

FIELD OBSERVATIONS

DATE/TIME OF DAY

LOCATION

WEATHER

SPECIES/DESCRIPTION

ACCOMPANIED BY

OBSERVATIONS

NOTES

SKETCHES

FIELD OBSERVATIONS

DATE/TIME OF DAY

LOCATION

WEATHER

SPECIES/DESCRIPTION

ACCOMPANIED BY

OBSERVATIONS

NOTES

SKETCHES

FIELD OBSERVATIONS

DATE/TIME OF DAY

LOCATION

WEATHER

SPECIES/DESCRIPTION

ACCOMPANIED BY

OBSERVATIONS

NOTES

SKETCHES

FIELD OBSERVATIONS

DATE/TIME OF DAY

LOCATION

WEATHER

SPECIES/DESCRIPTION

ACCOMPANIED BY

OBSERVATIONS

NOTES

SKETCHES

FIELD OBSERVATIONS

DATE/TIME OF DAY

LOCATION

WEATHER

SPECIES/DESCRIPTION

ACCOMPANIED BY

OBSERVATIONS

NOTES

SKETCHES

FIELD OBSERVATIONS

DATE/TIME OF DAY

LOCATION

WEATHER

SPECIES/DESCRIPTION

ACCOMPANIED BY

OBSERVATIONS

NOTES

SKETCHES

LISTEN—FOR AT such a moment your soul will be touched by sounds—to the soft, the mellow, the melting accents, which one might suppose inspired by Nature's self, and which she has taught the Ground Dove to employ in conveying the expression of his love to his mate, who is listening to them with delight.

—John James Audubon

FIELD OBSERVATIONS

DATE/TIME OF DAY

LOCATION

WEATHER

SPECIES/DESCRIPTION

ACCOMPANIED BY

OBSERVATIONS

NOTES

SKETCHES

FIELD OBSERVATIONS

DATE/TIME OF DAY

LOCATION

WEATHER

SPECIES/DESCRIPTION

ACCOMPANIED BY

OBSERVATIONS

NOTES

SKETCHES

FIELD OBSERVATIONS

DATE/TIME OF DAY

LOCATION

WEATHER

SPECIES/DESCRIPTION

ACCOMPANIED BY

OBSERVATIONS

NOTES

SKETCHES

FIELD OBSERVATIONS

DATE/TIME OF DAY

LOCATION

WEATHER

SPECIES/DESCRIPTION

ACCOMPANIED BY

OBSERVATIONS

NOTES

SKETCHES

FIELD OBSERVATIONS

DATE/TIME OF DAY

LOCATION

WEATHER

SPECIES/DESCRIPTION

ACCOMPANIED BY

OBSERVATIONS

NOTES

SKETCHES

FIELD OBSERVATIONS

DATE/TIME OF DAY

LOCATION

WEATHER

SPECIES/DESCRIPTION

ACCOMPANIED BY

OBSERVATIONS

NOTES

SKETCHES

FIELD OBSERVATIONS

DATE/TIME OF DAY

LOCATION

WEATHER

SPECIES/DESCRIPTION

ACCOMPANIED BY

OBSERVATIONS

NOTES

SKETCHES

FIELD OBSERVATIONS

DATE/TIME OF DAY

LOCATION

WEATHER

SPECIES/DESCRIPTION

ACCOMPANIED BY

OBSERVATIONS

NOTES

SKETCHES

FIELD OBSERVATIONS

DATE/TIME OF DAY

LOCATION

WEATHER

SPECIES/DESCRIPTION

ACCOMPANIED BY

OBSERVATIONS

NOTES

SKETCHES

FIELD OBSERVATIONS

DATE/TIME OF DAY

LOCATION

WEATHER

SPECIES/DESCRIPTION

ACCOMPANIED BY

OBSERVATIONS

NOTES

SKETCHES

FIELD OBSERVATIONS

DATE/TIME OF DAY

LOCATION

WEATHER

SPECIES/DESCRIPTION

ACCOMPANIED BY

OBSERVATIONS

NOTES

SKETCHES

FIELD OBSERVATIONS

DATE/TIME OF DAY

LOCATION

WEATHER

SPECIES/DESCRIPTION

ACCOMPANIED BY

OBSERVATIONS

NOTES

SKETCHES

HOW OFTEN, when snugly settled under the boughs of my temporary encampment . . . have I been saluted with the exulting bursts of this nightly disturber of the peace [the Barred Owl]—Its *whah, whah, whah, whah-a,* is uttered loudly, and in so strange and ludicrous a manner, that I should not be surprised were you to compare these sounds to the affected bursts of laughter which you may have heard from some of the fashionable members of your own species.

—John James Audubon

FIELD OBSERVATIONS

DATE/TIME OF DAY

LOCATION

WEATHER

SPECIES/DESCRIPTION

ACCOMPANIED BY

OBSERVATIONS

NOTES

SKETCHES

FIELD OBSERVATIONS

DATE/TIME OF DAY

LOCATION

WEATHER

SPECIES/DESCRIPTION

ACCOMPANIED BY

OBSERVATIONS

NOTES

SKETCHES

FIELD OBSERVATIONS

DATE/TIME OF DAY

LOCATION

WEATHER

SPECIES/DESCRIPTION

ACCOMPANIED BY

OBSERVATIONS

NOTES

SKETCHES

FIELD OBSERVATIONS

DATE/TIME OF DAY

LOCATION

WEATHER

SPECIES/DESCRIPTION

ACCOMPANIED BY

OBSERVATIONS

NOTES

SKETCHES

FIELD OBSERVATIONS

DATE/TIME OF DAY

LOCATION

WEATHER

SPECIES/DESCRIPTION

ACCOMPANIED BY

OBSERVATIONS

NOTES

SKETCHES

FIELD OBSERVATIONS

DATE/TIME OF DAY

LOCATION

WEATHER

SPECIES/DESCRIPTION

ACCOMPANIED BY

OBSERVATIONS

NOTES

SKETCHES

FIELD OBSERVATIONS

DATE/TIME OF DAY

LOCATION

WEATHER

SPECIES/DESCRIPTION

ACCOMPANIED BY

OBSERVATIONS

NOTES

SKETCHES

FIELD OBSERVATIONS

DATE/TIME OF DAY

LOCATION

WEATHER

SPECIES/DESCRIPTION

ACCOMPANIED BY

OBSERVATIONS

NOTES

SKETCHES

FIELD OBSERVATIONS

DATE/TIME OF DAY

LOCATION

WEATHER

SPECIES/DESCRIPTION

ACCOMPANIED BY

OBSERVATIONS

NOTES

SKETCHES

FIELD OBSERVATIONS

DATE/TIME OF DAY

LOCATION

WEATHER

SPECIES/DESCRIPTION

ACCOMPANIED BY

OBSERVATIONS

NOTES

SKETCHES

FIELD OBSERVATIONS

DATE/TIME OF DAY

LOCATION

WEATHER

SPECIES/DESCRIPTION

ACCOMPANIED BY

OBSERVATIONS

NOTES

SKETCHES

FIELD OBSERVATIONS

DATE/TIME OF DAY

LOCATION

WEATHER

SPECIES/DESCRIPTION

ACCOMPANIED BY

OBSERVATIONS

NOTES

SKETCHES

THE GOLDEN-WINGED Woodpecker [Common Flicker] never suffers its naturally lively spirit to droop. By way of amusement, it will continue to destroy as much furniture in a day as can well be handled by a different kind of workman or two.

—John James Audubon

FIELD OBSERVATIONS

DATE/TIME OF DAY

LOCATION

WEATHER

SPECIES/DESCRIPTION

ACCOMPANIED BY

OBSERVATIONS

NOTES

SKETCHES

FIELD OBSERVATIONS

DATE/TIME OF DAY

LOCATION

WEATHER

SPECIES/DESCRIPTION

ACCOMPANIED BY

OBSERVATIONS

NOTES

SKETCHES

FIELD OBSERVATIONS

DATE/TIME OF DAY

LOCATION

WEATHER

SPECIES/DESCRIPTION

ACCOMPANIED BY

OBSERVATIONS

NOTES

SKETCHES

FIELD OBSERVATIONS

DATE/TIME OF DAY

LOCATION

WEATHER

SPECIES/DESCRIPTION

ACCOMPANIED BY

OBSERVATIONS

NOTES

SKETCHES

FIELD OBSERVATIONS

DATE/TIME OF DAY

LOCATION

WEATHER

SPECIES/DESCRIPTION

ACCOMPANIED BY

OBSERVATIONS

NOTES

SKETCHES

FIELD OBSERVATIONS

DATE/TIME OF DAY

LOCATION

WEATHER

SPECIES/DESCRIPTION

ACCOMPANIED BY

OBSERVATIONS

NOTES

SKETCHES

FIELD OBSERVATIONS

DATE/TIME OF DAY

LOCATION

WEATHER

SPECIES/DESCRIPTION

ACCOMPANIED BY

OBSERVATIONS

NOTES

SKETCHES

FIELD OBSERVATIONS

DATE/TIME OF DAY

LOCATION

WEATHER

SPECIES/DESCRIPTION

ACCOMPANIED BY

OBSERVATIONS

NOTES

SKETCHES

FIELD OBSERVATIONS

DATE/TIME OF DAY

LOCATION

WEATHER

SPECIES/DESCRIPTION

ACCOMPANIED BY

OBSERVATIONS

NOTES

SKETCHES

FIELD OBSERVATIONS

DATE/TIME OF DAY

LOCATION

WEATHER

SPECIES/DESCRIPTION

ACCOMPANIED BY

OBSERVATIONS

NOTES

SKETCHES

FEW BIRDS exhibit a more affectionate disposition than the little Redpoll [Common Redpoll (Lesser Red-poll)], and it was pleasing to see several on a twig feeding each other and passing a seed from bill to bill, one individual sometimes receiving food from his two neighbors at the same time.

—John James Audubon

FIELD OBSERVATIONS

DATE/TIME OF DAY

LOCATION

WEATHER

SPECIES/DESCRIPTION

ACCOMPANIED BY

OBSERVATIONS

NOTES

SKETCHES

ADDITIONAL NOTES

ADDITIONAL NOTES

ADDITIONAL NOTES

LIFE LIST

Ducks, Geese, and Swans (Anatidae)

○ Black-bellied Whistling-Duck
○ Fulvous Whistling-Duck
○ Greater White-fronted Goose
○ Emperor Goose
○ Snow Goose
○ Ross's Goose
○ Brant
○ Cackling Goose
○ Canada Goose
○ Mute Swan
○ Trumpeter Swan
○ Mute Swan
○ Tundra Swan
○ Whooper Swan
○ Wood Duck
○ Gadwall
○ Eurasian Wigeon
○ American Wigeon
○ American Black Duck
○ Mallard
○ Mottled Duck
○ Blue-winged Teal
○ Cinnamon Teal
○ Northern Shoveler
○ Northern Pintail
○ Green-winged Teal
○ Canvasback
○ Redhead
○ Steller's Eider
○ Spectacled Eider

LIFE LIST

- ○ King Eider
- ○ Common Eider
- ○ Harlequin Duck
- ○ White-winged Scoter
- ○ Black Scoter
- ○ Long-tailed Duck
- ○ Bufflehead
- ○ Common Goldeneye
- ○ Barrow's Goldeneye
- ○ Hooded Merganser
- ○ Common Merganser
- ○ Red-breasted Merganser
- ○ Masked Duck
- ○ Ruddy Duck

Curassows and Guans (Cracidae)

- ○ Plain Chachalaca

Partridges, Grouse, Turkeys, and Old World Quail (Phasianidae)

- ○ Chukar
- ○ Gray Partridge
- ○ Ring-necked Pheasant
- ○ Ruffed Grouse
- ○ Greater Sage-Grouse
- ○ Gunnison Sage-Grouse
- ○ Spruce Grouse
- ○ Willow Ptarmigan
- ○ Rock Ptarmigan
- ○ White-tailed Ptarmigan
- ○ Blue Grouse
- ○ Sharp-tailed Grouse

LIFE LIST

SPECIES	DATE	LOCATION	P. Nº
○ Greater Prairie-Chicken			
○ Lesser Prairie-Chicken			
○ Wild Turkey			

New World Quail (Odontophoridae)

○ Mountain Quail			
○ Scaled Quail			
○ California Quail			
○ Gambel's Quail			
○ Northern Bobwhite			
○ Montezuma Quail			

Loons (Gaviidae)

○ Red-throated Loon			
○ Arctic Loon			
○ Pacific Loon			
○ Common Loon			
○ Yellow-billed Loon			

Grebes (Podicipedidae)

○ Least Grebe			
○ Pied-billed Grebe			
○ Horned Grebe			
○ Red-necked Grebe			
○ Eared Grebe			
○ Western Grebe			
○ Clark's Grebe			

Shearwaters and Petrels (Procellariidae)

○ Northern Fulmar			
○ Black-capped Petrel			

SPECIES	DATE	LOCATION	P. Nº
○ Cory's Shearwater			
○ Pink-footed Shearwater			
○ Flesh-footed Shearwater			
○ Greater Shearwater			
○ Buller's Shearwater			
○ Sooty Shearwater			
○ Short-tailed Shearwater			
○ Manx Shearwater			
○ Black-vented Shearwater			
○ Audubon's Shearwater			

Storm Petrels (Hydrobatidae)

○ Wilson's Storm Petrel			
○ Fork-tailed Storm Petrel			
○ Leach's Storm Petrel			
○ Ashy Storm Petrel			
○ Black Storm Petrel			
○ Least Storm Petrel			

Tropicbirds (Phaethontidae)

○ White-tailed Tropicbird			
○ Red-billed Tropicbird			

Boobies and Gannets (Sulidae)

○ Masked Booby			
○ Blue-footed Booby			
○ Brown Booby			
○ Red-footed Booby			
○ Northern Gannet			

LIFE LIST

Pelicans (Pelecanidae)

○ American White Pelican
○ Brown Pelican

Cormorants (Phalacrocoracidae)

○ Brandt's Cormorant
○ Neotropic Cormorant
○ Double-crested Cormorant
○ Great Cormorant
○ Red-faced Cormorant
○ Pelagic Cormorant

Darters (Anhingidae)

○ Anhinga

Frigatebirds (Fregatidae)

○ Magnificent Frigatebird
○ Great Frigatebird
○ Lesser Frigatebird

Bitterns, Herons, and Allies (Ardeidae)

○ American Bittern
○ Least Bittern
○ Great Blue Heron
○ Great Egret
○ Snowy Egret
○ Little Blue Heron
○ Tricolored Heron
○ Reddish Egret
○ Cattle Egret
○ Green Heron

LIFE LIST

○ Black-crowned Night-Heron
○ Yellow-crowned Night-Heron

Ibises and Spoonbills (Threskiornithidae)

○ White Ibis
○ Scarlet Ibis
○ Glossy Ibis
○ White-faced Ibis
○ Roseate Spoonbill

Storks (Ciconiidae)

○ Wood Stork

New World Vultures (Cathartidae)

○ Black Vulture
○ Turkey Vulture
○ California Condor

Hawks, Kites, Eagles, and Allies (Accipitridae)

○ Osprey
○ Hook-billed Kite
○ Swallow-tailed Kite
○ White-tailed Kite
○ Snail Kite
○ Mississippi Kite
○ Bald Eagle
○ Northern Harrier
○ Sharp-shinned Hawk
○ Cooper's Hawk
○ Northern Goshawk
○ Gray Hawk

LIFE LIST

- ○ Common Black-Hawk
- ○ Harris's Hawk
- ○ Roadside Hawk
- ○ Red-shouldered Hawk
- ○ Broad-winged Hawk
- ○ Short-tailed Hawk
- ○ Swainson's Hawk
- ○ White-tailed Hawk
- ○ Zone-tailed Hawk
- ○ Red-tailed Hawk
- ○ Ferruginous Hawk
- ○ Rough-legged Hawk
- ○ Golden Eagle

Caracaras and Falcons (Falconidae)

- ○ Crested Caracara
- ○ American Kestrel
- ○ Merlin
- ○ Aplomado Falcon
- ○ Gyrfalcon
- ○ Peregrine Falcon
- ○ Prairie Falcon

Rails, Gallinules, and Coots (Rallidae)

- ○ Black Rail
- ○ Clapper Rail
- ○ King Rail
- ○ Virginia Rail
- ○ Sora
- ○ Purple Gallinule
- ○ Common Moorhen

LIFE LIST

SPECIES	DATE	LOCATION	P. №
○ American Coot			

Limpkins (Aramidae)

○ Limpkin			

Cranes (Gruidae)

○ Sandhill Crane			
○ Whooping Crane			

Lapwings and Plovers (Charadriidae)

○ Black-bellied Plover			
○ American Golden-Plover			
○ Pacific Golden-Plover			
○ Snowy Plover			
○ Wilson's Plover			
○ Semipalmated Plover			
○ Piping Plover			
○ Killdeer			
○ Mountain Plover			

Oystercatchers (Haematopodidae)

○ American Oystercatcher			
○ Black Oystercatcher			

Stilts and Avocets (Recurvirostridae)

○ Black-necked Stilt			
○ American Avocet			

Sandpipers, Phalaropes, and Allies (Scolopacidae)

○ Greater Yellowlegs			
○ Lesser Yellowlegs			

LIFE LIST

SPECIES	DATE	LOCATION	P. Nº
○ Solitary Sandpiper			
○ Willet			
○ Spotted Sandpiper			
○ Upland Sandpiper			
○ Whimbrel			
○ Bristle-thighed Curlew			
○ Long-billed Curlew			
○ Hudsonian Godwit			
○ Bar-tailed Godwit			
○ Marbled Godwit			
○ Ruddy Turnstone			
○ Black Turnstone			
○ Surfbird			
○ Red Knot			
○ Sanderling			
○ Semipalmated Sandpiper			
○ Western Sandpiper			
○ Least Sandpiper			
○ White-rumped Sandpiper			
○ Baird's Sandpiper			
○ Pectoral Sandpiper			
○ Purple Sandpiper			
○ Rock Sandpiper			
○ Dunlin			
○ Curlew Sandpiper			
○ Stilt Sandpiper			
○ Buff-breasted Sandpiper			
○ Ruff			
○ Short-billed Dowitcher			
○ Long-billed Dowitcher			
○ Wilson's Snipe			

LIFE LIST

- ○ American Woodcock
- ○ Wilson's Phalarope
- ○ Red-necked Phalarope
- ○ Red Phalarope

Skuas, Gulls, Terns, and Skimmers (Laridae)

- ○ Great Skua
- ○ South Polar Skua
- ○ Pomarine Jaeger
- ○ Parasitic Jaeger
- ○ Long-tailed Jaeger
- ○ Laughing Gull
- ○ Franklin's Gull
- ○ Little Gull
- ○ Black-headed Gull
- ○ Bonaparte's Gull
- ○ Heermann's Gull
- ○ Mew Gull
- ○ Ring-billed Gull
- ○ California Gull
- ○ Herring Gull
- ○ Thayer's Gull
- ○ Iceland Gull
- ○ Lesser Black-backed Gull
- ○ Western Gull
- ○ Glaucous-winged Gull
- ○ Glaucous Gull
- ○ Great Black-backed Gullf
- ○ Sabine's Gull
- ○ Black-legged Kittiwake
- ○ Red-legged Kittiwake

LIFE LIST

SPECIES	DATE	LOCATION	P. №
○ Ross's Gull			
○ Ivory Gull			
○ Gull-billed Tern			
○ Caspian Tern			
○ Royal Tern			
○ Elegant Tern			
○ Sandwich Tern			
○ Roseate Tern			
○ Common Tern			
○ Arctic Tern			
○ Forster's Tern			
○ Least Tern			
○ Bridled Tern			
○ Sooty Tern			
○ Black Tern			
○ Brown Noddy			
○ Black Skimmer			

Auks, Murres, and Puffins (Alcidae)

○ Dovekie			
○ Common Murre			
○ Thick-billed Murre			
○ Razorbill			
○ Black Guillemot			
○ Pigeon Guillemot			
○ Marbled Murrelet			
○ Kittlitz's Murrelet			
○ Xantus's Murrelet			
○ Craveri's Murrelet			
○ Ancient Murrelet			
○ Cassin's Auklet			

LIFE LIST

SPECIES	DATE	LOCATION	P. Nº
○ Parakeet Auklet			
○ Least Auklet			
○ Crested Auklet			
○ Rhinoceros Auklet			
○ Atlantic Puffin			
○ Horned Puffin			
○ Tufted Puffin			

Pigeons and Doves (Columbidae)

○ Rock Pigeon			
○ Scaly-naped Pigeon			
○ White-crowned Pigeon			
○ Red-billed Pigeon			
○ Band-tailed Pigeon			
○ Eurasian Collared-Dove			
○ Spotted Dove			
○ White-winged Dove			
○ Zenaida Dove			
○ Mourning Dove			
○ Inca Dove			
○ Common Ground-Dove			

Lories, Parakeets, Macaws, and Parrots (Psittacidae)

○ Monk Parakeet			
○ Green Parakeet			
○ Thick-billed Parrot			
○ White-winged Parakeet			
○ Yellow-chevroned Parakeet			
○ Red-crowned Parrot			

LIFE LIST

Cuckoos, Roadrunners, and Anis (Cuculidae)

- ○ Black-billed Cuckoo
- ○ Yellow-billed Cuckoo
- ○ Mangrove Cuckoo
- ○ Greater Roadrunner
- ○ Smooth-billed Ani
- ○ Groove-billed Ani

Barn Owls (Tytonidae)

- ○ Barn Owl

Typical Owls (Strigidae)

- ○ Flammulated Owl
- ○ Western Screech-Owl
- ○ Eastern Screech-Owl
- ○ Whiskered Screech-Owl
- ○ Great Horned Owl
- ○ Snowy Owl
- ○ Northern Hawk Owl
- ○ Northern Pygmy-Owl
- ○ Ferruginous Pygmy-Owl
- ○ Elf Owl
- ○ Burrowing Owl
- ○ Barred Owl
- ○ Great Gray Owl
- ○ Long-eared Owl
- ○ Short-eared Owl
- ○ Boreal Owl
- ○ Northern Saw-whet Owl

LIFE LIST

Goatsuckers (Caprimulgidae)

- ○ Lesser Nighthawk
- ○ Common Nighthawk
- ○ Common Pauraque
- ○ Common Poorwill
- ○ Chuck-will's-widow
- ○ Whip-poor-will

Swifts (Apodidae)

- ○ Black Swift
- ○ Chimney Swift
- ○ Vaux's Swift
- ○ White-throated Swift

Hummingbirds (Trochilidae)

- ○ Broad-billed Hummingbird
- ○ White-eared Hummingbird
- ○ Berylline Hummingbird
- ○ Buff-bellied Hummingbird
- ○ Violet-crowned Hummingbird
- ○ Blue-throated Hummingbird
- ○ Magnificent Hummingbird
- ○ Lucifer Hummingbird
- ○ Ruby-throated Hummingbird
- ○ Black-chinned Hummingbird
- ○ Anna's Hummingbird
- ○ Costa's Hummingbird
- ○ Calliope Hummingbird
- ○ Broad-tailed Hummingbird
- ○ Rufous Hummingbird
- ○ Allen's Hummingbird

LIFE LIST

Trogons (Trogonidae)

- ○ Elegant Trogon
- ○ Eared Quetzal

Kingfishers (Alcedinidae)

- ○ Ringed Kingfisher
- ○ Belted Kingfisher
- ○ Green Kingfisher

Woodpeckers and Allies (Picidae)

- ○ Lewis's Woodpecker
- ○ Red-headed Woodpecker
- ○ Acorn Woodpecker
- ○ Gila Woodpecker
- ○ Golden-fronted Woodpecker
- ○ Red-bellied Woodpecker
- ○ Williamson's Sapsucker
- ○ Yellow-bellied Sapsucker
- ○ Red-naped Sapsucker
- ○ Red-breasted Sapsucker
- ○ Ladder-backed Woodpecker
- ○ Nuttall's Woodpecker
- ○ Downy Woodpecker
- ○ Hairy Woodpecker
- ○ Arizona Woodpecker
- ○ Red-cockaded Woodpecker
- ○ White-headed Woodpecker
- ○ American Three-toed Woodpecker
- ○ Black-backed Woodpecker
- ○ Northern Flicker
- ○ Gilded Flicker

SPECIES	DATE	LOCATION	P. NO
○ Pileated Woodpecker			

Tyrant Flycatchers (Tyrannidae)

SPECIES	DATE	LOCATION	P. NO
○ Northern Beardless-Tyrannulet			
○ Olive-sided Flycatcher			
○ Greater Pewee			
○ Western Wood-Pewee			
○ Eastern Wood-Pewee			
○ Yellow-bellied Flycatcher			
○ Acadian Flycatcher			
○ Alder Flycatcher			
○ Willow Flycatcher			
○ Least Flycatcher			
○ Hammond's Flycatcher			
○ Gray Flycatcher			
○ Dusky Flycatcher			
○ Pacific-slope Flycatcher			
○ Cordilleran Flycatcher			
○ Buff-breasted Flycatcher			
○ Black Phoebe			
○ Eastern Phoebe			
○ Say's Phoebe			
○ Vermilion Flycatcher			
○ Dusky-capped Flycatcher			
○ Ash-throated Flycatcher			
○ Great Crested Flycatcher			
○ Brown-crested Flycatcher			
○ Great Kiskadee			
○ Tropical Kingbird			
○ Couch's Kingbird			
○ Cassin's Kingbird			

LIFE LIST

- ○ Thick-billed Kingbird
- ○ Western Kingbird
- ○ Eastern Kingbird
- ○ Gray Kingbird
- ○ Scissor-tailed Flycatcher
- ○ Fork-tailed Flycatcher

Shrikes (Laniidae)

- ○ Loggerhead Shrike
- ○ Northern Shrike

Vireos (Vireonidae)

- ○ White-eyed Vireo
- ○ Bell's Vireo
- ○ Black-capped Vireo
- ○ Gray Vireo
- ○ Yellow-throated Vireo
- ○ Plumbeous Vireo
- ○ Cassin's Vireo
- ○ Blue-headed Vireo
- ○ Hutton's Vireo
- ○ Warbling Vireo
- ○ Philadelphia Vireo
- ○ Red-eyed Vireo
- ○ Yellow-green Vireo
- ○ Black-whiskered Vireo

Jays and Crows (Corvidae)

- ○ Gray Jay
- ○ Steller's Jay
- ○ Blue Jay

LIFE LIST

- ○ Green Jay
- ○ Florida Scrub-Jay
- ○ Island Scrub-Jay
- ○ Western Scrub-Jay
- ○ Mexican Jay
- ○ Pinyon Jay
- ○ Clark's Nutcracker
- ○ Black-billed Magpie
- ○ Yellow-billed Magpie
- ○ American Crow
- ○ Northwestern Crow
- ○ Fish Crow
- ○ Chihuahuan Raven
- ○ Common Raven

Larks (Alaudidae)

- ○ Horned Lark

Swallows (Hirundinidae)

- ○ Purple Martin
- ○ Tree Swallow
- ○ Violet-green Swallow
- ○ Northern Rough-winged Swallow
- ○ Bank Swallow
- ○ Cliff Swallow
- ○ Cave Swallow
- ○ Barn Swallow

Chickadees and Titmice (Paridae)

- ○ Carolina Chickadee
- ○ Black-capped Chickadee

LIFE LIST

SPECIES	DATE	LOCATION	P. №
○ Mountain Chickadee			
○ Mexican Chickadee			
○ Chestnut-backed Chickadee			
○ Boreal Chickadee			
○ Gray-headed Chickadee			
○ Bridled Titmouse			
○ Oak Titmouse			
○ Juniper Titmouse			
○ Tufted Titmouse			
○ Black-crested Titmouse			

Verdins (Remizidae)

○ Verdin

Bushtits (Aegithalidae)

○ Bushtit

Nuthatches (Sittidae)

○ Red-breasted Nuthatch
○ White-breasted Nuthatch
○ Pygmy Nuthatch
○ Brown-headed Nuthatch

Creepers (Certhiidae)

○ Brown Creeper

Wrens (Troglodytidae)

○ Cactus Wren
○ Rock Wren
○ Canyon Wren
○ Carolina Wren

LIFE LIST

○ Bewick's Wren
○ House Wren
○ Winter Wren
○ Sedge Wren
○ Marsh Wren

Dippers (Cinclidae)

○ American Dipper

Kinglets (Regulidae)

○ Golden-crowned Kinglet
○ Ruby-crowned Kinglet

Old World Warblers and Gnatcatchers (Sylviidae)

○ Arctic Warbler
○ Blue-gray Gnatcatcher
○ California Gnatcatcher
○ Black-tailed Gnatcatcher

Thrushes (Turdidae)

○ Bluethroat
○ Northern Wheatear
○ Eastern Bluebird
○ Western Bluebird
○ Mountain Bluebird
○ Townsend's Solitaire
○ Veery
○ Gray-cheeked Thrush
○ Bicknell's Thrush
○ Swainson's Thrush
○ Hermit Thrush

LIFE LIST

SPECIES	DATE	LOCATION	P. Nº
○ Wood Thrush			
○ American Robin			
○ Varied Thrush			

Babblers (Timaliidae)

○ Wrentit			

Mockingbirds and Thrashers (Mimidae)

○ Gray Catbird			
○ Northern Mockingbird			
○ Sage Thrasher			
○ Brown Thrasher			
○ Bendire's Thrasher			
○ Curve-billed Thrasher			
○ California Thrasher			
○ Crissal Thrasher			
○ Le Conte's Thrasher			

Starlings (Sturnidae)

○ European Starling			

Wagtails and Pipits (Motacillidae)

○ Eastern Yellow Wagtail			
○ Citrine Wagtail			
○ Red-throated Pipit			
○ American Pipit			
○ Sprague's Pipit			

Waxwings (Bombycillidae)

○ Bohemian Waxwing			
○ Cedar Waxwing			

LIFE LIST

Silky flycatchers (Ptilogonatidae)

○ Phainopepla

Olive Warblers (Peucedramidae)

○ Olive Warbler

Wood-Warblers (Parulidae)

○ Blue-winged Warbler
○ Golden-winged Warbler
○ Tennessee Warbler
○ Orange-crowned Warbler
○ Nashville Warbler
○ Virginia's Warbler
○ Colima Warbler
○ Lucy's Warbler
○ Northern Parula
○ Tropical Parula
○ Yellow Warbler
○ Chestnut-sided Warbler
○ Magnolia Warbler
○ Cape May Warbler
○ Black-throated Blue Warbler
○ Yellow-rumped Warbler
○ Black-throated Gray Warbler
○ Golden-cheeked Warbler
○ Black-throated Green Warbler
○ Townsend's Warbler
○ Hermit Warbler
○ Blackburnian Warbler
○ Yellow-throated Warbler
○ Grace's Warbler

LIFE LIST

- ○ Pine Warbler
- ○ Kirtland's Warbler
- ○ Prairie Warbler
- ○ Palm Warbler
- ○ Bay-breasted Warbler
- ○ Blackpoll Warbler
- ○ Cerulean Warbler
- ○ Black-and-white Warbler
- ○ American Redstart
- ○ Prothonotary Warbler
- ○ Worm-eating Warbler
- ○ Swainson's Warbler
- ○ Ovenbird
- ○ Northern Waterthrush
- ○ Louisiana Waterthrush
- ○ Kentucky Warbler
- ○ Connecticut Warbler
- ○ Mourning Warbler
- ○ MacGillivray's Warbler
- ○ Common Yellowthroat
- ○ Hooded Warbler
- ○ Wilson's Warbler
- ○ Canada Warbler
- ○ Red-faced Warbler
- ○ Painted Redstart
- ○ Yellow-breasted Chat

Tanagers (Thraupidae)

- ○ Hepatic Tanager
- ○ Summer Tanager
- ○ Scarlet Tanager

LIFE LIST

○ Western Tanager

Emberizids (Emberizidae)

○ Olive Sparrow
○ Green-tailed Towhee
○ Spotted Towhee
○ Eastern Towhee
○ Canyon Towhee
○ California Towhee
○ Abert's Towhee
○ Cassin's Sparrow
○ Bachman's Sparrow
○ Rufous-crowned Sparrow
○ American Tree Sparrow
○ Chipping Sparrow
○ Clay-colored Sparrow
○ Brewer's Sparrow
○ Field Sparrow
○ Black-chinned Sparrow
○ Vesper Sparrow
○ Lark Sparrow
○ Black-throated Sparrow
○ Sage Sparrow
○ Lark Bunting
○ Savannah Sparrow
○ Grasshopper Sparrow
○ Baird's Sparrow
○ Henslow's Sparrow
○ Conte's Sparrow
○ Nelson's Sharp-tailed Sparrow
○ Saltmarsh Sharp-tailed Sparrow

LIFE LIST

- ◯ Seaside Sparrow
- ◯ Fox Sparrow
- ◯ Song Sparrow
- ◯ Lincoln's Sparrow
- ◯ Swamp Sparrow
- ◯ White-throated Sparrow
- ◯ Harris's Sparrow
- ◯ White-crowned Sparrow
- ◯ Golden-crowned Sparrow
- ◯ Dark-eyed Junco
- ◯ Yellow-eyed Junco
- ◯ McCown's Longspur
- ◯ Lapland Longspur
- ◯ Smith's Longspur
- ◯ Chestnut-collared Longspur
- ◯ Snow Bunting
- ◯ McKay's Bunting

Cardinals, Saltators, and Allies (Cardinalidae)

- ◯ Northern Cardinal
- ◯ Pyrrhuloxia
- ◯ Rose-breasted Grosbeak
- ◯ Black-headed Grosbeak
- ◯ Blue Grosbeak
- ◯ Lazuli Bunting
- ◯ Indigo Bunting
- ◯ Varied Bunting
- ◯ Painted Bunting
- ◯ Dickcissel

LIFE LIST

Blackbirds (Icteridae)

○ Bobolink
○ Red-winged Blackbird
○ Tricolored Blackbird
○ Eastern Meadowlark
○ Western Meadowlark
○ Yellow-headed Blackbird
○ Rusty Blackbird
○ Brewer's Blackbird
○ Common Grackle
○ Boat-tailed Grackle
○ Great-tailed Grackle
○ Shiny Cowbird
○ Bronzed Cowbird
○ Brown-headed Cowbird
○ Orchard Oriole
○ Hooded Oriole
○ Bullock's Oriole
○ Altamira Oriole
○ Audubon's Oriole
○ Baltimore Oriole
○ Scott's Oriole

Finches and Allies (Fringillidae)

○ Gray-crowned Rosy-Finch
○ Black Rosy-Finch
○ Brown-capped Rosy-Finch
○ Pine Grosbeak
○ Purple Finch
○ Cassin's Finch
○ House Finch

LIFE LIST

SPECIES	DATE	LOCATION	P. Nº
○ Red Crossbill			
○ White-winged Crossbill			
○ Common Redpoll			
○ Hoary Redpoll			
○ Pine Siskin			
○ Lesser Goldfinch			
○ Lawrence's Goldfinch			
○ American Goldfinch			
○ Evening Grosbeak			

Old World Sparrows (Passeridae)

○ House Sparrow			

AMERICAN BIRDING ASSOCIATION CODE OF BIRDING ETHICS

1. Promote the welfare of birds and their environment.

1(a) Support the protection of important bird habitat.

1(b) To avoid stressing birds or exposing them to danger, exercise restraint and caution during observation, photography, sound recording, or filming.

Limit the use of recordings and other methods of attracting birds, and never use such methods in heavily birded areas or for attracting any species that is Threatened, Endangered, of Special Concern, or is rare in your local area.

Keep well back from nests and nesting colonies, roosts, display areas, and important feeding sites. In such sensitive areas, if there is a need for extended observation, photography, filming, or recording, try to use a blind or hide, and take advantage of natural cover.

Use artificial light sparingly for filming or photography, especially for close-ups.

1(c) Before advertising the presence of a rare bird, evaluate the potential for disturbance to the bird, its surroundings, and other people in the area, and proceed only if access can be controlled, disturbance minimized, and permission has been obtained from private land-owners. The sites of rare nesting birds should be divulged only to the proper conservation authorities.

1(d) Stay on roads, trails, and paths where they exist; otherwise, keep habitat disturbance to a minimum.

2. Respect the law, and the rights of others.

2(a) Do not enter private property without the owner's explicit permission.

2(b) Follow all laws, rules, and regulations governing use of roads and public areas, both at home and abroad.

2(c) Practice common courtesy in contacts with other people. Your exemplary behavior will generate goodwill with birders and non-birders alike.

3. Ensure that feeders, nest structures, and other artificial bird environments are safe.

3(a) Keep dispensers, water, and food clean and free of decay or disease. It is important to feed birds continually during harsh weather.

3(b) Maintain and clean nest structures regularly.

3(c) If you are attracting birds to an area, ensure the birds are not exposed to predation from cats and other domestic animals or dangers posed by artificial hazards.

4. Group birding, whether organized or impromptu, requires special care.

Each individual in the group, in addition to the obligations spelled out in Items #1 and #2, has responsibilities as a Group Member:

4(a) Respect the interests, rights, and skills of fellow birders, as well as people participating in other legitimate outdoor activities. Freely share your knowledge and experience, except where code 1(c) applies. Be especially helpful to beginning birders.

4(b) If you witness unethical birding behavior, assess the situation and intervene if you think it prudent. When interceding, inform the person(s) of the inappropriate action and attempt, within reason, to have it stopped. If the behavior continues, document it and notify appropriate individuals or organizations.

Group Leader Responsibilities [amateur and professional trips and tours]:

4(c) Be an exemplary ethical role model for the group. Teach through word and example.

4(d) Keep groups to a size that limits impact on the environment and does not interfere with others using the same area.

4(e) Ensure everyone in the group knows of and practices this code.

4(f) Learn and inform the group of any special circumstances applicable to the areas being visited (e.g., no audio playback allowed).

4(g) Acknowledge that professional tour companies bear a special responsibility to place the welfare of birds and the benefits of public knowledge ahead of the company's commercial interests. Ideally, leaders should keep track of tour sightings, document unusual occurrences, and submit records to appropriate organizations.

Please Follow this Code and Distribute and Teach it to Others

The American Birding Association's Code of Birding Ethics may be freely reproduced for distribution/dissemination. Visit aba.org for more information about the American Birding Association.